To Patty

God richly bless you with the sweet, quiet spirit.

Love Sheila Warren
2017

Devotions at Sunset

SHEILA WARREN

WESTBOW PRESS
A DIVISION OF THOMAS NELSON
& ZONDERVAN

Copyright © 2017 Sheila Warren.

All rights reserved. No part of this book may be used or reproduced by any means, graphic, electronic, or mechanical, including photocopying, recording, taping or by any information storage retrieval system without the written permission of the author except in the case of brief quotations embodied in critical articles and reviews.

Scripture taken from the New King James Version®. Copyright © 1982 by Thomas Nelson. Used by permission. All rights reserved.

Scripture quotations are taken from the Holy Bible, New Living Translation, copyright ©1996, 2004, 2007, 2013, 2015 by Tyndale House Foundation. Used by permission of Tyndale House Publishers, Inc., Carol Stream, Illinois 60188. All rights reserved.

Scriptures marked KJV are taken from the KING JAMES VERSION (KJV): KING JAMES VERSION, public domain.

WestBow Press books may be ordered through booksellers or by contacting:

WestBow Press
A Division of Thomas Nelson & Zondervan
1663 Liberty Drive
Bloomington, IN 47403
www.westbowpress.com
1 (866) 928-1240

Because of the dynamic nature of the Internet, any web addresses or links contained in this book may have changed since publication and may no longer be valid. The views expressed in this work are solely those of the author and do not necessarily reflect the views of the publisher, and the publisher hereby disclaims any responsibility for them.

Any people depicted in stock imagery provided by Thinkstock are models, and such images are being used for illustrative purposes only.
Certain stock imagery © Thinkstock.

ISBN: 978-1-5127-6690-5 (sc)
ISBN: 978-1-5127-6689-9 (e)

Library of Congress Control Number: 2016920135

Print information available on the last page.

WestBow Press rev. date: 3/20/2017

CONTENTS

Week 1: Love 1
Week 2: Praise 2
Week 3: Compassion 3
Week 4: Quietness 4
Week 5: Self-Control 5
Week 6: Confidence 6
Week 7: Alone but Not Lonely 7
Week 8: Peace 9
Week 9: Trust 10
Week 10: Bless 11
Week 11: Fear 12
Week 12: Forgiveness 13
Week 13: Knowledge 14
Week 14: Hope 15
Week 15: Give/Giving/Giver 17
Week 16: Hear 18
Week 17: Strength 19
Week 18: Defense 20
Week 19: Pray 21
Week 20: Thanks/Thankful/Thanksgiving 23

Week 21: Obedience 24
Week 22: Prosperity 25
Week 23: Diligence 26
Week 24: Patience 27
Week 25: Walking 29
Week 26: Healing/Healed 30
Week 27: Wisdom 31
Week 28: Waiting/Wait 32
Week 29: Mercy/Mercies 33
Week 30: Kindness 35
Week 31: Righteousness 36
Week 32: Truth 37
Week 33: Joy 38
Week 34: Power 39
Week 35: Exhort 41
Week 36: Revelations 42
Week 37: Faith 43
Week 38: Steadfast 44
Week 39: Lead 45
Week 40: Watch 47
Week 41: Vanity 48
Week 42: Rejoice! 49
Week 43: Proud 50
Week 44: Endure 51
Week 45: Delight 52
Week 46: Salvation 53
Week 47: Rest 55
Week 48: Disobedience 56

Week 49: Humility 57
Week 50: Holiness 58
Week 51: Submit 59
Week 52: Riches 60

Week 1
LOVE

John 15:11–14 NKJV
Jesus said, "These things I have spoken to you, that my joy may remain in you, and that your joy may be full. This is my commandment, that you love one another as I have loved you. Greater love has no-one than this, than to lay down one's life for his friends. You are my friends if you do whatever I command."

Note
I believe that when we encourage someone, whether a relative, a friend or even a stranger, our action truly touches the heart of God. We would make God happy—no *joyful*—if we loved each other as much as *He* loves us. Jesus laid down *His* life for all of us! *Think about it!* We cannot outdo love.

Week 2
PRAISE

Psalm 22:3 NKJV
"But You are holy, who inhabit the praises of Israel [His people]."

Psalm 34:1 NKJV
"I will bless the Lord at all times; His praise shall continually be in my mouth."

Note
Just think about it, wherever and whenever we are praising God, there He is! He is in our midst. We should always be praising God in song, speaking of His goodness, acknowledging our lives in Him. Recently a cashier was undercharging me $20 for my purchase. I pointed out the error, and she was very thankful. I said, "I cannot call myself a Christian and be dishonest." I felt that was a praise (shout-out) to the Lord.

Week 3

COMPASSION

Psalm 145:8 NKJV
"The Lord is gracious, and full of compassion; slow to anger, and of great mercy."

Note
Recently I heard a pastor explaining that he felt deep compassion well up within him for a very sick person because she was determined to be healed. And she was healed! While watching the news, I had such compassion for a lady I saw crying because her daughter had been killed by a hit-and-run driver. It was so sad; I could not watch the news any longer. The dictionary – (Webster's 1983 edition) defines *compassion* as "showing pity and *merciful*."

Week 4

QUIETNESS

1 Timothy 2:1–2 NKJV
"Therefore, I exhort first of all that supplications, prayers, intercessions, and giving thanks to be made for all men, for kings and all who are in authority, that we may lead a quiet and peaceable life in all godliness and reverence."

Note

Have you ever noticed that the quieter you are, the more you can and do become still? I am able to hear from God more clearly when I grow quiet. I get new and fresh ideas, and some of my problems become solutions! I certainly feel a stronger sense of God's presence; it quite often brings me to tears. In this atmosphere, I feel so protected. Jesus is truly beautiful!

Week 5

SELF-CONTROL

Psalm 81:10 NKJV
"I am the Lord your God, who brought you out of the land of Egypt; open your mouth wide and I will fill it."

Note

The biggest problem we have with self-control is controlling our mouths. If we read and study the Bible, which is God's Word and allow God to fill our mouths, we will have powerful and meaningful things to share. We would not have half of the problems we have with one another. Words from God build up and do not pull down. Sometimes it is difficult to maintain self-control in some situations, but God's Word will enable us to be more than conquerors through Christ Jesus. Have your way, Lord!

Week 6
CONFIDENCE

Proverbs 14:26 NKJV
"In the fear [respect] of the Lord there is strong confidence. And His children will have a place of refuge."

Philippians 1:6 NKJV
"Being confident of this very thing, that He who has begun a good work in you will complete it until the day of Jesus Christ."

Note
God's Word is so reassuring. As long as we fear and respect God, as long as we trust in Him, He has promised to be our refuge. And He never breaks His promises. Yes, we can hide in Him and have no doubt that He will continue to work on and with us until He comes again. God is awesome!

Week 7

ALONE BUT NOT LONELY

Hebrews 13:5b NKJV
"For He Himself has said, 'I will never leave you nor forsake you.'"

Note

Jesus was never lonely, because the Father was with Him as the hour drew near. We need not be lonely either. Remember what Jesus said about His Father: He will never leave us or forsake us. He is always with us by His Holy Spirit. He is always ready and willing to help us in any situation. He is our helper. There is nothing people can do to us that God cannot undo. When we accept Him as our saviour, He lives in us. He never lets us down and always remains true to His Word.

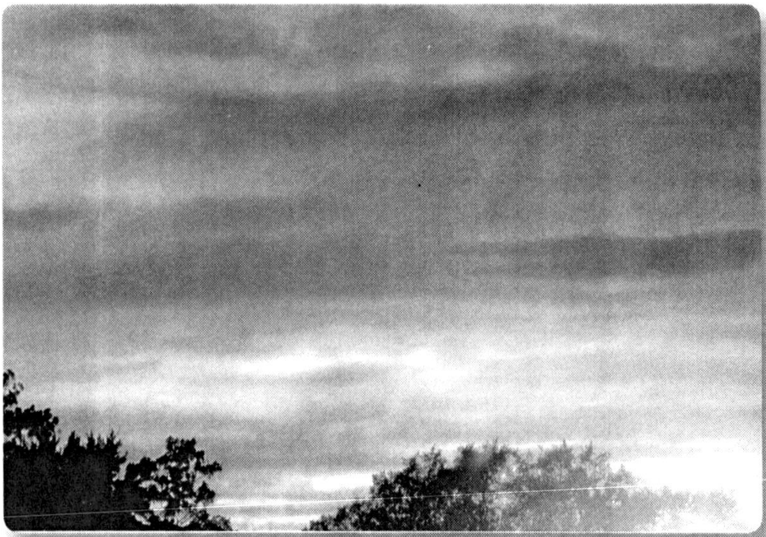

Week 8
PEACE

John 16:33 NKJV (emphasis added)
"These things I have spoken to you, that in *Me*, you may have peace. In the world you will have tribulation; but be of good cheer, I have overcome the world!"

Note
Thanks be to God in Jesus's name! *He* has overcome the world. There is *nothing* for us to be overly concerned about. We are to pray, trust God and do what we can to better the situations around us. We can have perfect peace. Leave the rest to Jesus, the author and finisher of our faith!

Week 9
TRUST

Proverbs 3:5–6 NKJV (emphasis added)
"Trust in the Lord with *all* your heart, and lean not on your own understanding. In *all* your ways acknowledge Him, and He will direct your paths."

Note

God made each one of us. He has a perfect, individualized plan for our lives. That is why we can trust Him in *all* things. Sometimes, especially when we are young, if we are honest with ourselves, we can admit that we see people we admire and want to emulate. Many times, we miss out on who and what God has in mind for us as an individual because we are busy trying to be like other people. Let's each be the person God has made us to be. His plans are far greater and better than ours.

Week 10
BLESS

Psalm 103:1–2 NKJV (emphasis added)
"Bless the Lord, O my soul; and *all* that is within me, bless His holy name! Bless the Lord, oh my soul, and forget not all His benefits."

Note

When the scripture says "*all* that is within," I believe that means *all* of my muscles, bones, blood, organs, mind, and so on—"all that is within me." And when someone does you wrong, ask God to bless that person. The Word of God does say, "Many are the afflictions of the righteous, but the Lord delivers him out of them all" (Psalm 34:19 NKJV). Very often, we hear it said that we were made to be blessed and to be a blessing. I totally agree.

Week 11
FEAR

Proverbs 3:24–26 NKJV
"When you lie down, you will not be afraid; yes, you will lie down and your sleep will be sweet. Do not be afraid of sudden terror, nor of trouble from the wicked when it comes. For the Lord will be your confidence. And will keep your foot from being caught."

Note
I have heard it said that fear is *false evidence appearing real*. Some lives are built on fear—the fear of not being good enough or not being accepted by others, the fear of all of the terrible things going on in the world, and on and on. Fear is not of God. He said He has not given us the spirit of fear but of love, power and a sound mind. So, if you are not looking to Jesus, you would have an unsound mind.

Week 12

FORGIVENESS

Ephesians 4:32 NKJV
"And be kind to one another, tenderhearted, forgiving one another, even as God in Christ also forgave you."

Note

This week, make a conscious effort to be tender-hearted and forgiving to everyone you meet. Do not expect this to be easy all the time. It does not matter if the people you encounter are family, friends or complete strangers. Just forgive, forget, and get over it, whatever *it* is. When I was young, my mother often said, "Forgive and forget." I guess that is why it has been easy over the years to forgive.

Week 13
KNOWLEDGE

Proverbs 1:7 NKJV
"The fear [respect] of the Lord is the beginning of knowledge, but fools despise wisdom and instruction."

Note
When I was seeking God in prayer, I asked what I should write regarding knowledge. Suddenly He answered, "Knowledge is bliss." (*Webster's Dictionary* – 1983 edition) defines *bliss* as "the acme of happiness; heavenly rapture, supremely happy." The more knowledge you have about the true and living God, the more freedom you will have from religion and the closer your personal relationship with God will become.

Week 14
HOPE

Psalm 71:5 NKJV
"For you are my hope, O Lord God; You are my trust from my youth."

Titus 1:2 NKJV
"In hope of eternal life which God, who cannot lie, promised before time began."

Note
Knowing that we can trust God in every situation gives us great hope. Hope inspires us to praise God more and more. It also gives us peace, knowing that God has promised to give us eternal life if we accept Jesus as our Lord and Saviour and live according to His will.

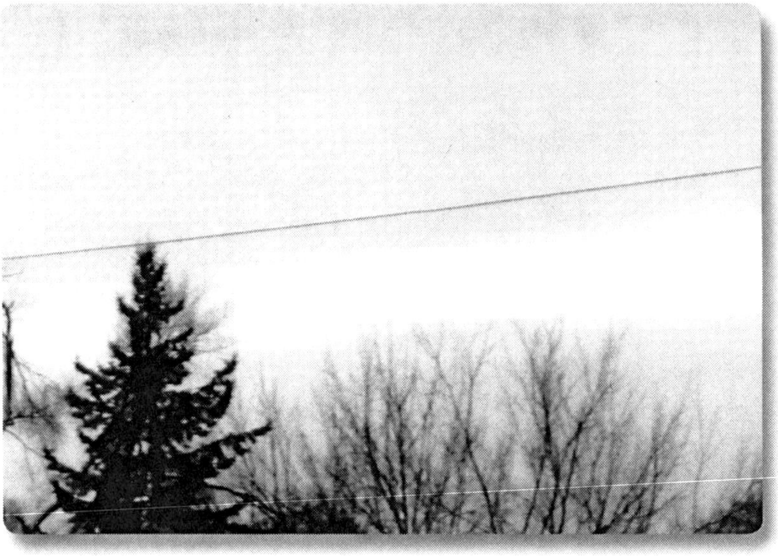

Week 15

GIVE/GIVING/GIVER

2 Corinthians 9:7 NKJV
"So let each one give as he purposes in his heart, not grudgingly or of necessity; for God loves a cheerful giver."

Note
When you do not feel like giving, it may be because God does not want you to give to that person or ministry at that time. God does give us joy and peace regarding whom to give to and the exact time. Ask, "Lord, help me not to be a grumpy giver." Remember to thank God at all times!

Week 16
HEAR

John 10:27 NKJV
"My sheep hear My voice, and I know them, and they follow Me."

Note
Many years ago, before I accepted Jesus into my life, I heard an audible voice giving me an instruction. I did not obey. Of course, there were many consequences. In later years, I asked the Lord, "Why did I not obey?" and immediately the thought came to me: *My sheep hear my voice.* Jesus knocks at our heart's door, and until we allow Him to come into our hearts and lives, we cannot reap the benefits. Have you accepted Him yet?

Week 17
STRENGTH

Mark 12:29–30 NKJV
"Jesus answered him, 'The first of all the commandments is: Hear, O Israel, the Lord our God, the Lord is one. And you shall love the Lord your God with all your heart, with all your soul, with all your mind, and with all your strength. This is the first commandment.'"

Note
God is *the* God. We are to have no other gods. We are to worship the true and living God—no images or any likenesses. We are not to use God's name as a curse word. That is what this command means to me—to love Him, with all my heart, soul, mind and strength!

Week 18
DEFENSE

Psalm 62:6 NKJV
"He only is my rock and my salvation; He is my defense; I shall not be moved."

Note
Because Jesus is our rock, salvation, and defense, we do not have to worry and stress ourselves in any situation that may arise. Nothing beats prayer, waiting and watching. *He* will defend and direct us! Be patient and trust in Him.

Week 19
PRAY

Mark 11:24 NKJV
"Therefore I say to you, whatever things you ask when you pray, believe that you receive them, and you will have them."

Note

It is great if you can get someone you trust to agree with you in prayer. The scripture does say, "If any two agree on earth concerning anything that they ask it will be done for them by my Father in Heaven" (Matthew 18:19). Prayer can and should be done anytime—morning, noon and night. Wherever you are, you can offer a silent prayer to God. Sometimes "lifting Holy hands, without wrath or doubting" (1 Timothy 2:8).

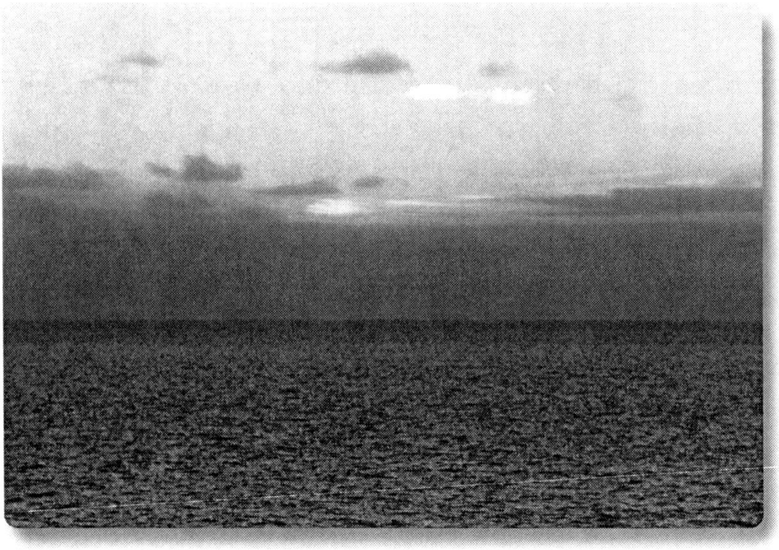

Week 20
THANKS/THANKFUL/THANKSGIVING

1 Chronicles 16:34a NKJV
"Oh, give thanks to the Lord for He is good! For His mercy endures forever."

Note
We can and should be thankful *in* every situation—not *for* every situation. Some situations can be very painful. We can always be thankful *in* every situation, because we can be sure that as we trust God, it will be worked out in our favour. We give thanks to God because He is good and His mercy is forever and ever. He always provides for us, if we trust Him even when our faith is wavering. He always has our backs, always!

Week 21
OBEDIENCE

Romans 5:19 NKJV
"For as by one man's disobedience many were made sinners, so also by one Man's obedience many will be made righteous."

Note

Adam and Eve sinned against God, which caused us to become sinners. Thank God He sent Jesus to the cross in our place, to redeem or save us from our sins. This has given us, believers in Jesus Christ, the opportunity to receive eternal life. It is also our responsibility to introduce Jesus Christ to as many people as possible, wherever and whenever we can.

Week 22
PROSPERITY

Psalm 118:25 NKJV
"Save now, I pray, O Lord; O Lord, I pray, send now prosperity."

Note
God always hears and answers our prayers. His timing is perfect. We do not need to be anxious if we have a bill to pay or an expense. He is always on time. If we ask for prosperity, we can be sure it will come, usually when most needed but least expected.

Week 23

DILIGENCE

2 Peter 1:5–8 NKJV
But also for this very reason, giving all diligence, add to your faith virtue, to virtue knowledge, to knowledge self-control, to self-control perseverance, to perseverance godliness, to godliness brotherly kindness, to brotherly kindness love. For if these things are yours and abound, you will be neither barren nor unfruitful in the knowledge of our Lord Jesus Christ.

Note
If we diligently seek to know Jesus and His ways, we will become full of the knowledge of Him and how He expects us to live our lives. Practising diligence and persevering in whatever we do, we can be certain that our efforts will be blessed.

Week 24
PATIENCE

James 1:2–3 NKJV
"My brethren, count it all joy when you fall into various trials, knowing that the testing of your faith produces patience."

Note
I once read that we should not ask God for patience because we will receive more tribulation! In my experience, asking God for patience and taking a deep breath bring a certain level of peace. I always thank God for the peace that patience can bring.

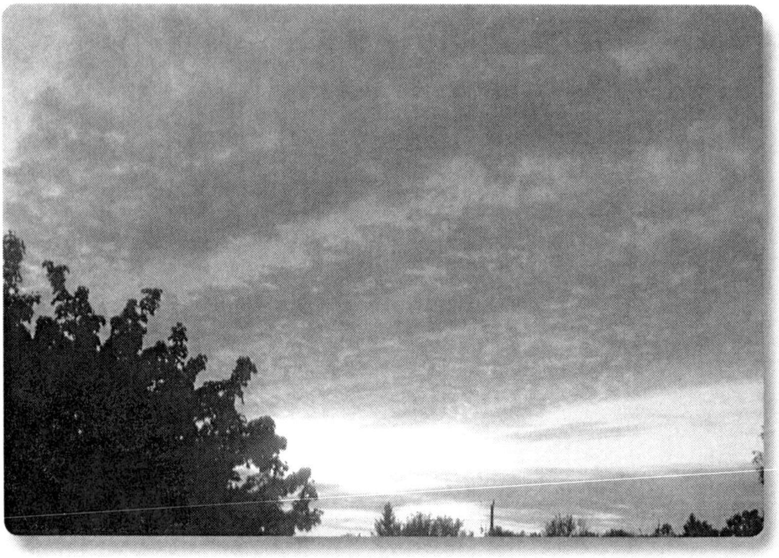

Week 25
WALKING

Acts 9:31 NKJV
"Then the churches throughout all Judea, Galilee, and Samaria had peace and were edified. And walking, in the fear [respect] of the Lord and in the comfort of the Holy Spirit, they were multiplied."

Note
These churches were and are very good examples to other churches. They had peace, improved their minds and morals, and walked in the respect of the Lord and in the comfort of the Holy Spirit. This all brought increase to the churches.

Week 26
HEALING/HEALED

Psalm 107:20 NLT
"He sent His word and healed them, snatching them from the door of death."

Acts 4:22 KJV
"For the man was above forty years old, on whom this miracle of healing was shewed."

Note
We can believe God's Word, the Bible, just has to be sent forth (near and far) and people can be healed! Being of a certain age is not a criterion. With Jesus, age does not matter. God said in Deuteronomy 7:15, "And the Lord will take away from you all sickness," so we can expect healing, because God promised. And that is one of the reasons that Jesus died on the cross of Calvary.

Week 27
WISDOM

James 1:5–6 NKJV
"If any of you lacks wisdom, let him ask of God, who gives to all liberally and without reproach, and it will be given to him. But let him ask in faith, with no doubting, for he who doubts is like a wave of the sea driven and tossed by the wind."

Note
There will be times in life when we just do not know what to do. When I was writing this devotional, sometimes I had a mental block. God wants us to trust Him for the answers we need. He may use someone in the process to reveal something to you. Refrain from asking everyone else before putting your question to God. God always has the best answer.

Week 28
WAITING/WAIT

Psalm 27:14 NKJV
"Wait on the Lord; be of good courage. And He shall strengthen your heart; wait I say on the Lord!"

Note
God does not want us to be anxious about anything. He said to "wait." When we get discouraged and do things our own way in a hasty fashion, we usually make big mistakes. And there are always consequences. It is always wise to wait on the Lord.

Week 29

MERCY/MERCIES

Lamentations 3:22–23 NKJV
"Through the Lord's mercies we are not consumed, because His compassions fail not. They are new every morning; great is your faithfulness."

Note
Let's remember to thank God for His mercies, which are forever and new every morning!

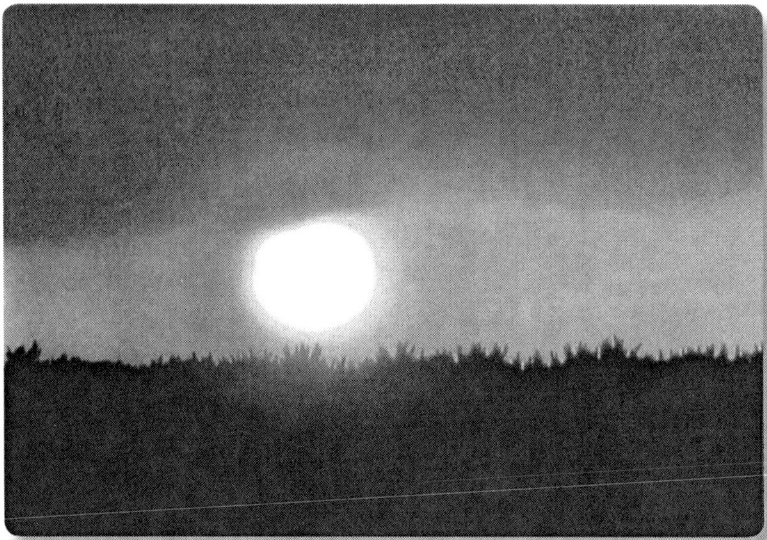

Week 30
KINDNESS

Nehemiah 9:17 NKJV
"They refused to obey … But you are God, ready to pardon, gracious and merciful, slow to anger, abundant in kindness, and did not forsake them."

Note
Lord, we thank You for Your salvation, which we received through Your grace in Jesus Christ. Although we are sometimes disobedient, You are always forgiving and kind to us. Our kindness to one another will also produce love.

Week 31
RIGHTEOUSNESS

Proverbs 14:34 NKJV

"Righteousness exalts a nation, but sin is a reproach to any people."

Note

You may be certain that if you determine to live your life in a godly manner, God Almighty is going to bless you in His own way.

A nation that conducts itself by using Godly principles will be elevated to the highest degree by God and will be respected by other nations worldwide. In Jesus's name.

Week 32
TRUTH

John 8:32 NKJV
"And you will know the truth, and the truth will set you free."

John 14:6 NLT
"Jesus told him, 'I am the way, the truth and the life. No one can come to the Father [God] except through me.'"

Note
Total freedom comes from knowing Jesus as Lord and Saviour. Try absolute truth for one year. I guarantee your life will change for the better. Nothing the government or our cultures say or do contrary to God's truths will last. God's truths through Jesus will be here forever! Amen.

Week 33
JOY

Psalm 16:11 NKJV
"You will show me the path of life; In your presence is fullness of joy; At your right hand are pleasures forevermore."

Note

As we experience all kinds of life challenges, sorrows and sudden changes, we should not allow sorrow and disappointment to pull us down totally. Where God's presence is, there is the fullness of joy and His strength. Our God has a solution to every problem, and it is good. He has pleasures for us forever.

Week 34
POWER

Acts 1:8 NLT
"But you will receive power when the Holy Spirit comes upon you. And you will be my witnesses, telling people about me everywhere—in Jerusalem, throughout Judea, in Samaria, and to the ends of the earth."

2 Timothy 1:7 NLT
"For God has not given us a spirit of fear, but of power and of love and of a sound mind."

Note
With the power that the Holy Spirit gives us comes the boldness to spread the gospel wherever we go. Jesus said that after He left earth, the Father would send the Holy Spirit, who is the helper and the teacher. The spirit of fear should not have reign over us. Power, love and a sound mind will help us to be who God created us to be!

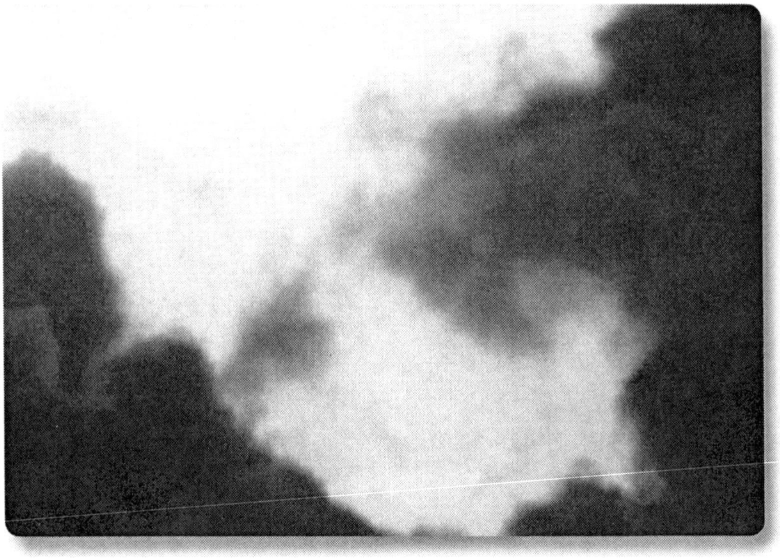

Week 35
EXHORT

1 Thessalonians 5:14 NKJV
"Now we exhort you, brethren, warn those who are unruly, comfort the fainthearted, uphold the weak, be patient with all."

Note

Exhort means to advise strongly (*Webster's Dictionary – 1983 Edition*). In these last days, how much more should we be exhorting Christians and non-Christians? Families are turning against each other, the governments are in upheaval, and lives are of no value with all sorts of killing. Things are all of a sudden considered wrong and not accepted and vice versa. We must get busy telling folks that Jesus never changes and about the *joy* of the Lord. He is the same yesterday, today and forevermore. We can have *joy* in the midst of all of our storms.

Week 36
REVELATIONS

Galatians 1:12 NLT
"I received my message from no human source, and no one taught me. Instead I received it by direct revelation from Jesus Christ."

Note

I have always had the desire to write. In my later years, I was contemplating writing a devotional. When talking with one of my sisters, I expressed this to her and she nonchalantly said, "Devotions at sunset." She knew that I love taking pictures of sunsets. I did not share this with anyone. Shortly after the conversation with my sister, I received a call from a friend from Florida. He said that the Lord had told him that I should be writing. This was a revelation to my sister and my friend and confirmation to me. I was surprised to say the least. That is when I slowly started writing. I was impressed to keep quiet until it was completed.

There is nothing better than receiving directly from Jesus because all good things come from Him! His time is not our time, and His ways are not our ways (Isaiah 55:8).

Week 37
FAITH

Romans 5:1 NKJV
"Therefore, having been justified by faith, we have peace with God through our Lord Jesus Christ."

James 2:26 NKJV
"For as the body without the spirit is dead, so faith without works is dead also."

Note
Jesus said that according to our faith, we will be healed—not according to the will of God. He wants us all to be healed. Through Jesus, we receive the peace that passes all understanding.

Week 38
STEADFAST

1 Corinthians 15:58 NKJV
"Therefore, my beloved brethren, be steadfast, immovable, always abounding in the work of the Lord, knowing that your labour is not in vain in the Lord."

Note
You can be very sure that whatever you do in the name of Jesus will be blessed. He will never give us an assignment that He is not willing or able to assist us with. You may get an idea to do something that you have never done or even thought of doing before, but Jesus is right there to help. Of course, you have to ask Him to help you. He said in the scriptures, "Call to me and I will answer you and show you great and mighty things which you do not know" (Jeremiah 33:3).

Week 39
LEAD

Psalm 139:24 NLT
"Point out anything in me that offends you, and lead me along the path of everlasting life."

Luke 6:39–40 NKJV
"And He spoke a parable to them: Can the blind lead the blind? Will they not both fall into the ditch? A disciple is not above his teacher, but everyone who is perfectly trained will be like his teacher."

Note
The greatest leader was Jesus. He was loving, kind, honest and understanding. We must be humble enough to go before God and ask for correction and direction, and He will lead us in the right direction. Proper leadership training will help us to become great leaders, pleasing to God. I learned many years ago that a good leader is good at delegating. Jesus did not do everything Himself; He had disciples to assist Him.

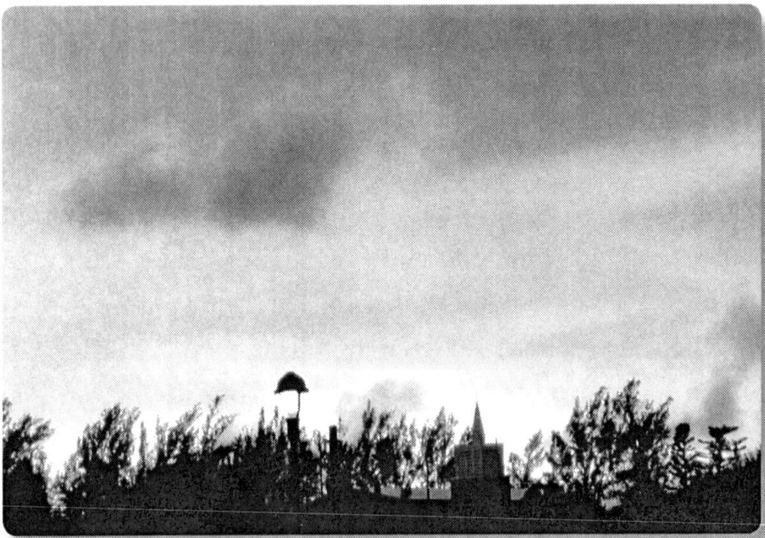

Week 40
WATCH

Psalm 141:3 NKJV
"Set a guard, O Lord, over my mouth. Keep watch over the door of my lips."

Note

I pray to be careful in what I say, especially when I am in a group of people. It is so very important that we speak in love. We could hurt a person and not be aware of it. He or she might not say anything. Most times, people do not say that you hurt them. Words can lift up, but they can also kill.

Week 41
VANITY

Psalm 144:4 KJV
"Man is like to vanity: his days are as a shadow that passes away."

Proverbs 13:11 KJV
"Wealth gotten by vanity shall be diminished: but he that gathereth by labour shall increase."

Note
Webster's Dictionary defines *vain* as useless, fruitless, empty, worthless, or conceited and *vanity* as something one is conceited about. Our lives are in God's hands. His time is not our time. It does not matter how wealthy we are. If God is absent in our lives, we are empty.

Week 42
REJOICE!

1 Chronicles 16:10 NKJV
"Glory in His holy name; let the hearts of those rejoice who seek the Lord!"

Note

We should rejoice and be happy, knowing that Jesus is coming again soon to take us home. He said that He is going to prepare a place for us and will come again. Until that time, we must continue, amid all of the hatred and violence, to win people to Jesus Christ.

Week 43
PROUD

James 4:6 NKJV
"But He gives more grace. Therefore He says: God resists the proud, but gives grace to the humble."

Note
It is very clear from the scriptures that God does not want us to be proud. In all of our efforts to keep pride out of our lives, God gives us more grace. Serving God is not based on the things that we *do not do*, but on the things that we *do*.

Week 44

ENDURE

2 Timothy 4:3 NKJV
"For the time will come when they will not endure sound doctrine, but according to their own desires, because they have itching ears, they will heap up for themselves teachers."

Note

Sometimes it is not easy following Jesus, but as God's Word says, we must endure to the end. The end is near when we see things being done just the opposite to what God instructed! Watch the daily news! People's consciences seem to be seared these days. There are so many killings. Life is not of much value anymore. And Jesus said He came to give us life and more abundantly.

Week 45
DELIGHT

Psalm 1:2 NKJV
"But his delight is in the law of the Lord, and in His law he meditates day and night."

Note

When we think on the things of God, we are more likely to want to please Him. When we pray with faith, we believe our Christian walk will be more stable and whatever we do will prosper.

Week 46

SALVATION

Acts 4:12 NLT

"There is salvation in no one else! God has given no other name under heaven by which we must be saved ..." [Jesus].

Note

Jesus was God in the flesh. He is the only one who died for us. We should take joy in the one who saved us from death to eternal life. If we accept Him as our Lord and Saviour, He will be our provider and healer. We can receive all that we need from Him.

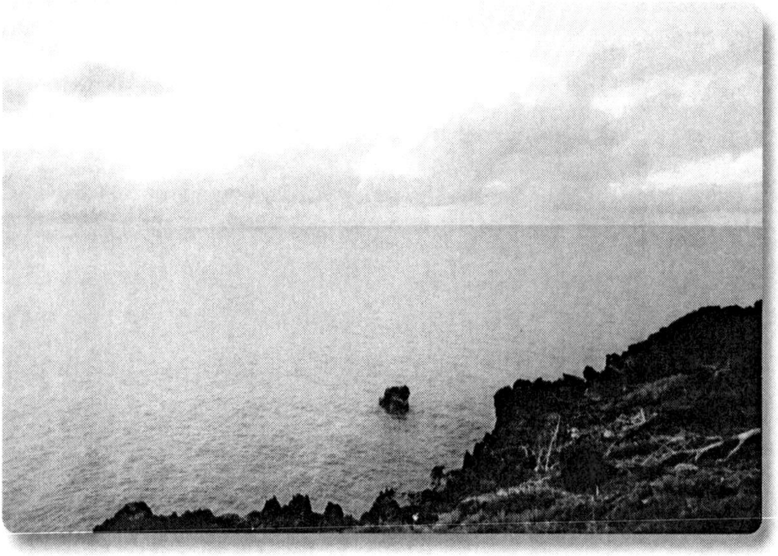

Week 47
REST

Psalm 37:7 NKJV
"Rest in the Lord, and wait patiently for Him; Do not fret because of him who prospers in his way, because of the man who brings wicked schemes to pass."

Note

God's time is perfect and pure. His ways are not our ways. He is always there for us. He promised to give us the desires of our hearts. I remember when I was a teenager, many years ago, I used to complain to my mother if I did not have what my friends had. She would always remind me that I did not know how others received what they had. Later I was thankful that she had told me that, because I learned that if I trust and rest in the Lord, I can and will have the things that I want and also need.

Week 48

DISOBEDIENCE

Romans 5:19 NKJV
"For as by one man's disobedience many were made sinners, so also by one man's obedience many will be made righteous."

Titus 3:3 NKJV
"For we ourselves were also once foolish, disobedient, deceived, serving various lusts and pleasures, living in malice and envy, hateful and hating one another."

Note
Thank You, Lord, for Jesus's obedience, which enables us to become righteous. By dying on the cross, He freed us from our disobedience, so that we could have a life filled with beauty. *Thank You, Jesus.*

Week 49

HUMILITY

Proverbs 15:33 NKJV
"The fear of the Lord is the instruction of wisdom, and before honour is humility."

Note
If we respect (fear) the Lord, we will receive humility, riches of all kinds, honour and life, as we are told in Proverbs 22:4.

Week 50
HOLINESS

Exodus 15:11 NKJV

"Who is like You, O Lord, among the gods? Who is like You, glorious in holiness, fearful in praises, doing wonders?"

Note

There is no one like the true and living God. No one can do wonders such as He. It is He who gives us rain and sunshine and heals all of our diseases. If we remain in a peaceful lifestyle, we will see Him in all of His glory. Hallelujah!

Week 51
SUBMIT

1 Peter 5:5 NKJV

"Likewise you younger people, submit yourselves to your elders. Yes, all of you be submissive to one another, and be clothed with humility, for "God resists the proud, but gives grace to the humble."

Note

There is an increase of ungodliness in our world today. God's Word, the Bible, has been turned around. More submission is in the devil's favour; that is why he is sticking around. When we submit to God and give no attention to the devil, he does not stay around us. Many of the young people in this generation do not read the Bible. We have to get back to reading the Bible and applying it to our lives.

Week 52
RICHES

1 Timothy 6:17 NKJV
"Command those who are rich in this present age not to be haughty, nor to trust in uncertain riches but in the living God, who gives us richly all things to enjoy."

Note
God is faithful in all things. He supplies all of our needs and lots of times our wants. Recently, I was praying about a financial situation, and the Holy Spirit whispered to me in His still, small voice, "It is just money." I thank God for that still, small voice, because the concern was not a concern any longer.